ROCKS AND GEMS

by Jaclyn Jaycox

PEBBLE
a capstone imprint

Read All About It is published by Pebble, an imprint of Capstone.
1710 Roe Crest Drive
North Mankato, Minnesota 56003
www.capstonepub.com

Library of Congress Cataloging-in-Publication Data is available on the Library of Congress website.
ISBN 978-1-9771-2529-3 (library binding)
ISBN 978-1-9771-2539-2 (eBook PDF)

Summary: Rocks and minerals are all around you. They are in your house, backyard, and even your food! Rocks are grouped into types, like sedimentary, igneous, and metamorphic. From some minerals, we get beautiful gemstones.

Image Credits
Getty Images: Mark Perlstein, top right 19; iStockphoto: Avdeev_80, middle 13, barmalini, 7, Radka Danailova, top 13, slobo, 12; Shutterstock: abid99, bottom 6, AlanMorris, top 21, Anatoli Styf, (red stone)Cover, Bas van der Pluijm, right 23, Bjoern Wylezich, bottom 18, BlackRabbit3, top 30, chittakorn59, right 1, corlaffra, 20, Doug McLean, bottom 29, Dr. Norbert Lange, top 27, Epitavi, top right Cover, es3n, bottom left 21, Famed01, top 5, Fokin Oleg, bottom 15, Freebulclicstar, top 17, HelenField, bottom 27, horiyan, bottom 10, Imfoto, middle 19, bottom 19, Inna Reznik, top 11, Ivaylo Ivanov, top 22, Jemastock, design element throughout, Jiri Hera, 8, ju_see, middle 17, Kelvin Degree, design element throughout, Kletr, top 25, LesPalenik, bottom 26, LuFeeTheBear, left 23, macy alexzandra villars, top 14, mangojuicy, top 29, Manutsawee Buapet, bottom 13, Noppanun K, design element throughout, Olga_Ionina, top 10, Paul Juser, top 15, Phil Woolley, bottom right 21, Photographee.eu, middle 14, Rasta777, bottom 22, ReVelStockArt, design elements throughout, Sebastian Janicki, 16, Serg64, top 6, Sergejus Lamanosovas, bottom 5, Shoot 24, 4, Steve Bower, left 24, StudioDin, bottom 9, Tatiana Popova, bottom 11, Tyler Boyes, bottom 25, bottom left 28, Vastram, middle 21, Victor Josan, top 9, Victor Moussa, top 18, Volonoff, design element throughout, vvoe, left 1, bottom 17, top 26, bottom 30, 31, Vyshedko, middle 30, Willyam Bradberry, right 24, Yury Kosourov, bottom right 28, Zaksheuskaya, (watercolor) Cover, design element; Wikimedia: KarlaPanchuk, bottom 14

Editorial Credits
Designer: Kayla Rossow; Media Researcher: Morgan Walters;
Production Specialist: Katy LaVigne

Printed and bound in China
PO3322

Table of Contents

Words in **bold** are in the glossary.

Chapter 1

What Are Rocks?

You've probably seen rocks scattered in the street. Or maybe you've skipped them across the water. But what do you know about them? Get ready to learn some cool things about rocks!

There are three kinds of rocks: sedimentary, igneous, and metamorphic.

sedimentary rock

Rocks are grouped together by what is in them and how they formed.

Rocks are made of two or more **minerals**. Minerals are made naturally in the earth.

There are more than 4,000 kinds of minerals.

metamorphic rock

5

Rocks are always changing.
They go through a cycle.
One kind of rock turns into
a different kind of rock.

igneous rock

Millions of years ago, humans
used rocks to make tools.

A mortar and pestle
is a grinding tool.

Long ago, women used ground up rocks as makeup.

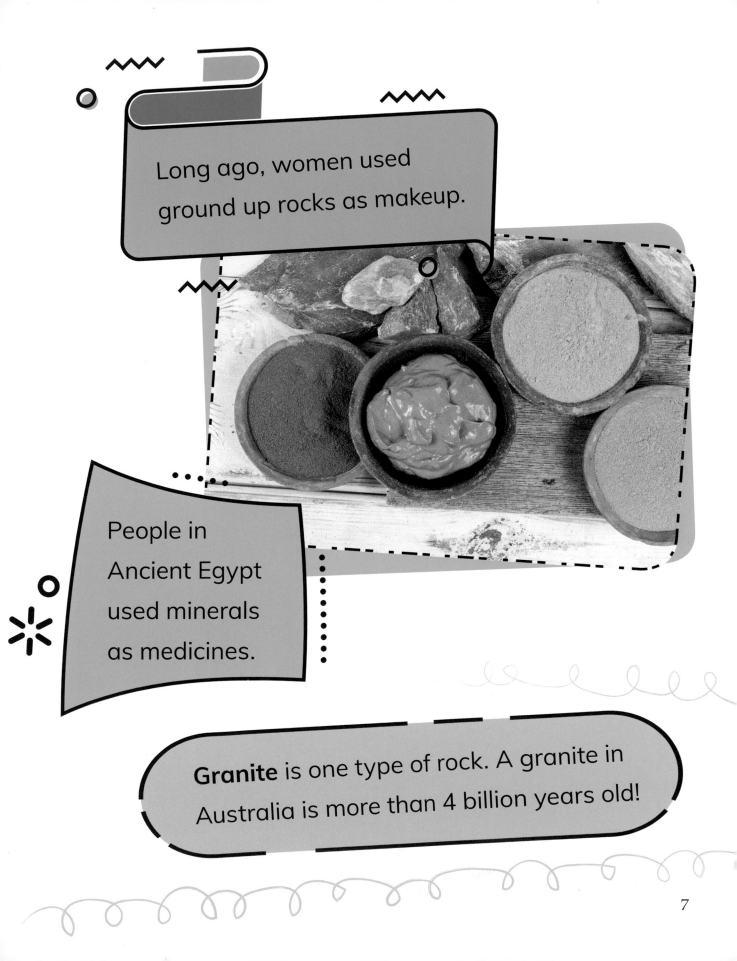

People in Ancient Egypt used minerals as medicines.

Granite is one type of rock. A granite in Australia is more than 4 billion years old!

Chapter 2

Rocks Are Everywhere!

You are never far away from rocks and minerals. They are in your home and at school. They are even in your food and drinks!

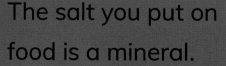

The salt you put on food is a mineral.

Earth's crust, the part we walk on, is made of rock.

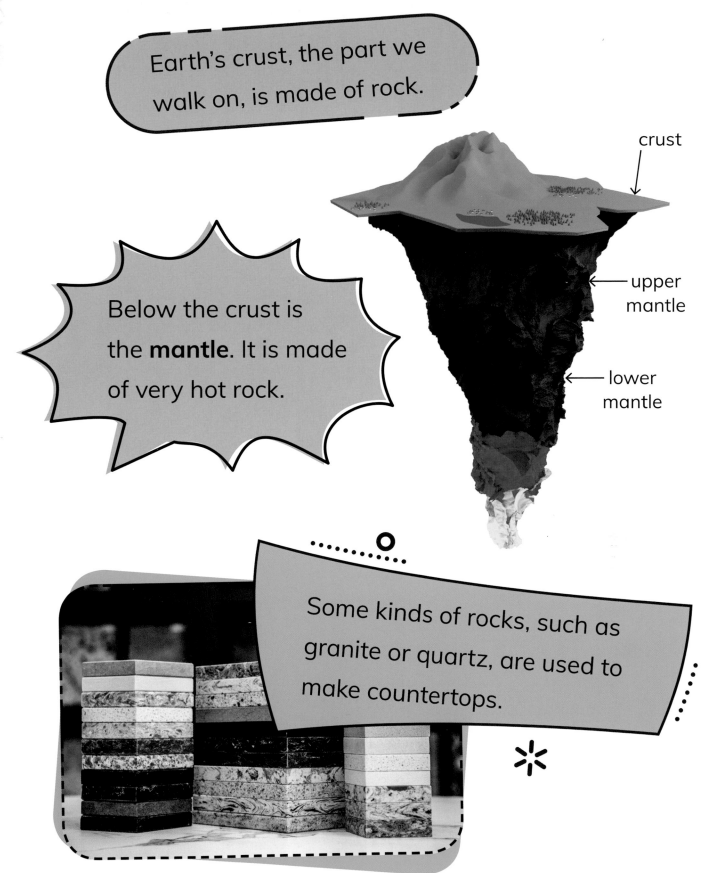

crust

upper mantle

lower mantle

Below the crust is the **mantle**. It is made of very hot rock.

Some kinds of rocks, such as granite or quartz, are used to make countertops.

Glass is made from sand. Sand is made of tiny rocks and minerals.

The lead in a pencil is a mineral called graphite.

Fluoride is a mineral. It is in toothpaste and helps keep teeth healthy.

Copper and lithium both come from minerals. They are used to make batteries.

Chapter 3

Properties of Rocks and Minerals

Physical properties are what you can see on rocks and minerals. They are used to sort rocks into different groups. They can also give you hints about which minerals rocks are made of.

Color is an easy property to see. Rocks can be any color. Some are even colorless.

Texture is how a rock feels. Some are bumpy and others are smooth.

Hardness is how easily a mineral can be scratched.

Mohs scale lists the hardness of 10 minerals. Diamonds are the hardest minerals in the world.

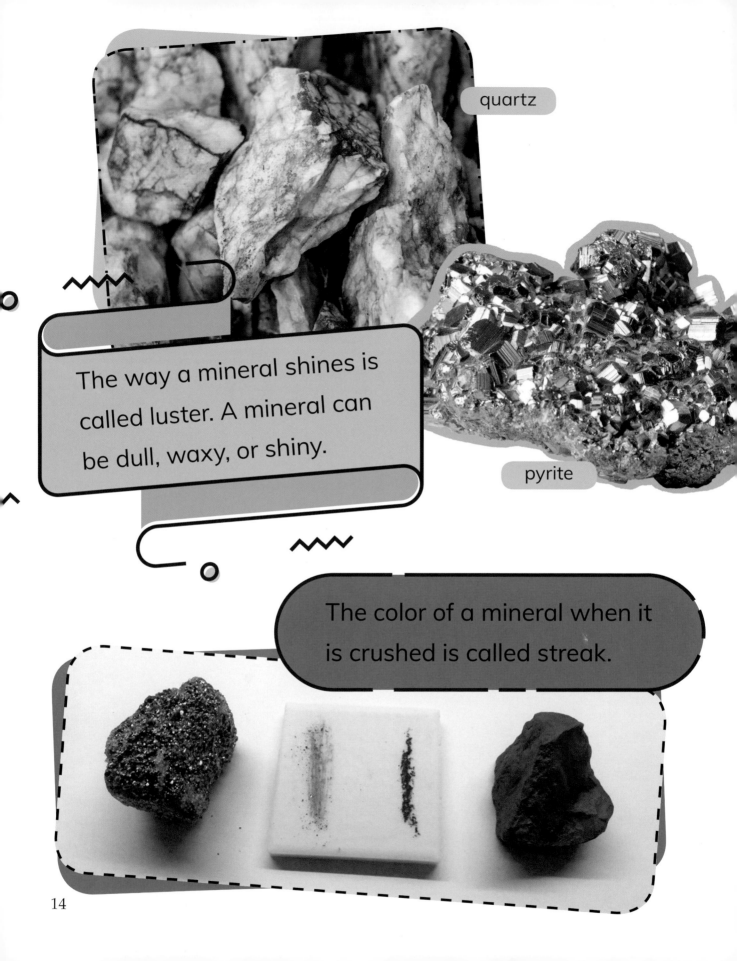

quartz

pyrite

The way a mineral shines is called luster. A mineral can be dull, waxy, or shiny.

The color of a mineral when it is crushed is called streak.

Minerals break differently. Some break into flat pieces. Some break into chunks.

shale

Tenacity is how hard it is to break or bend a rock or mineral.

antigorite

Chapter 4

Gemstones

Gemstones are **rare** minerals. They are usually very sparkly and pretty! Gemstones can be cut and cleaned. They are often made into jewelry.

Crystals form in minerals when they cool and become solid very slowly. Gems come from crystals.

celestite crystals

Most gemstones form in Earth's crust.

A gem's color comes from the **elements** it's made up of.

Many gemstones look like regular rocks until they are cut and cleaned.

There are five things needed to form a gemstone: ingredients, pressure, temperature, space, and time.

rubies

Diamonds come from Earth's mantle, where it is very hot. Diamonds need temperatures of at least 2,000 degrees Fahrenheit (1,093 degrees Celsius) to form.

The largest diamond found in the United States is called the Uncle Sam Diamond.

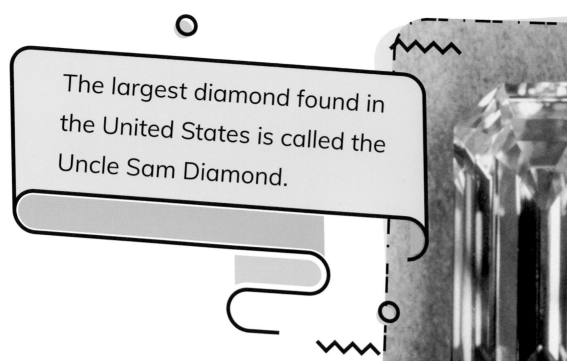

diamonds

The most valuable gemstones are called precious gems. They are diamonds, emeralds, sapphires, and rubies.

emeralds

Chapter 5

Sedimentary Rocks

Sediment is tiny pieces of rock. Wind or water washes it away. It becomes a layer of mud or sand. New sediment will pile on top and squish the layers below it, eventually turning it to rock.

Sediment also contains pieces of plants and animals.

Sedimentary rock is common at the bottom of lakes or oceans.

If you've ever seen stripes on the side of a cliff, that's sedimentary rock!

The layers in sedimentary rocks are called strata.

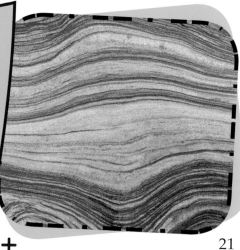

Coal and chalk are both sedimentary rocks.

chalk

coal

Fossils are most commonly found in sedimentary rock.

Scientists search sedimentary rock to learn about plants and animals that lived long ago.

fossils

Some types of sedimentary rock formed hundreds of millions of years ago!

Chapter 6

Igneous Rocks

Volcanoes help form igneous rocks. Igneous rocks are made from magma or lava. Magma is really hot rock found below Earth's surface. When it cools, it hardens.

Igneous rock can form either below or above Earth's surface.

molten lava

Devil's Tower in Wyoming is formed from igneous rock.

24

Rock formed above the surface is called extrusive igneous rock.

obsidian

Rock formed below the surface is called intrusive igneous rock.

diorite

Many mountains are made of igneous rock.

There are more than 700 different kinds of igneous rocks.

Granite is a type of igneous rock. It takes millions of years to form.

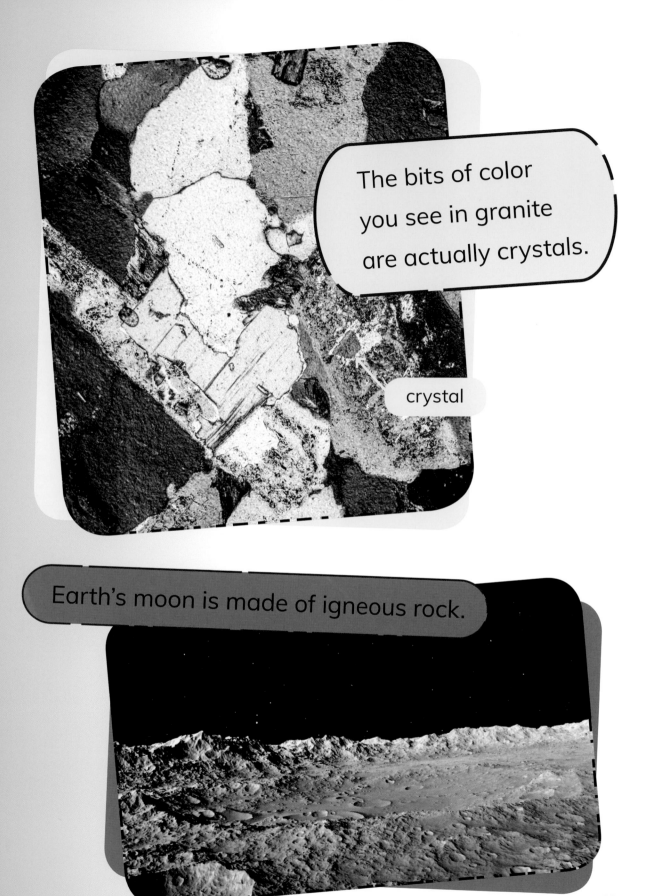

The bits of color you see in granite are actually crystals.

crystal

Earth's moon is made of igneous rock.

Chapter 7

Metamorphic Rocks

Metamorphic rocks start out as either sedimentary or igneous rocks. When they are exposed to lots of heat and pressure, they change. Metamorphic rocks are always changing.

slate

marble

Marble and slate are both metamorphic rocks.

Marble is made from limestone, a sedimentary rock.

limestone

Metamorphic means "to change form."

Metamorphic rock can change into different metamorphic rock.

Although metamorphic rock gets very hot, it doesn't melt.

There are two types of metamorphism: thermal and regional.

Slate is formed by regional metamorphism.

Hornfel is formed by thermal metamorphism.

Regional metamorphism happens when magma changes rock below Earth's surface.

Thermal metamorphism happens when magma changes rocks near Earth's surface.

Glossary

element—a substance that cannot be broken down into simpler substances

fossil—the remains or traces of an animal that lived millions of years ago

mantle—the part of a planet between the crust and the core

mineral—a solid found in nature that has a crystal structure

Mohs scale—a scale of hardness used in classifying minerals

rare—not often seen or found

sediment—a mixture of tiny bits of rock, shells, plants, sand, and minerals

texture—the way something feels

Index